Happy early 69th birthday, 2016

D0933746

THIS PRESENT MOMENT

# THIS PRESENT MOMENT

### NEW POEMS

## Gary Snyder

COUNTERPOINT

BERKELEY

Copyright © Gary Snyder 2015

All rights reserved under International and Pan-American Copyright Conventions.
No part of this book may be used or reproduced in any manner whatsoever without
written permission from the publisher, except in the case of brief quotations
embodied in critical articles and reviews.

Library of Congress Cataloging-in-Publication Data is available
ISBN 978-1-61902-524-0

Cover art by Tom Killion
Interior design and composition by David Bullen

COUNTERPOINT
2650 Ninth Street, Suite 318
Berkeley, CA 94710
www.counterpointpress.com

Printed in the United States of America
Distributed by Publishers Group West

10 9 8 7 6 5 4 3 2

For my fearless sister
Anthea Corinne Hogan Lowry Snyder

# Contents

# I. Outriders

## Gnarly

Splitting 18" long rounds from a beetle-kill
pine tree we felled
so it wouldn't smash a shed
— with a borrowed splitter briggs & stratton
twenty-ton pressure
wedge on a piston push-rod
some rounds fall clean down split in two,
some tough and thready, knotty,
full of frass and galleries, gnarly
gnarly! — my woman
                 she was sweet

## The Earth's Wild Places

Your eyes, your mouth and hands,
the public highways.
Hands, like truck stops,
semis rumbling in the corners.
Eyes like the bank clerk's window
foreign exchange.
I love all the parts of your body
friends hug your suburbs
farmlands are given a nod
but I know the path
to your wilderness.
It's not that I like it best,
but we're almost always
alone there,
and it's scary but also calm.

## Siberian Outpost

What are these deserts? Sheep overgrazed them years ago?
A sweeping gallery forest and a gentle five mile ridge of foxtail pine

Tom and I walk up the arid slope

Caught in lightning crashes —
Siberian Outpost meadow
bunchgrass tufts and gopher holes —
shelter in the space beneath a huge old edge-zone foxtail pine;
hail storm and heavy showers;
big root trees, red bark chunks — stay barely dry

*Lifetimes ago this same tree sheltered me*
*on Thornapple Island.*
*I was a junior bodhisattva then named*
*"No More Tricks"*
*and was sent to sit with the boulders here*
 *an aeon or two*
*til the soil came up to my eyes.*
*I shook and yanked and stood, said,*

OK Tom let's head back to the camp

*The desert smells like rain*

*2 August 2007  /  8 VIII  08*

## Walking the Long and Shady Elwha

After many years the two dams on the Elwha River of the Olympic Peninsula came down. The Elwha Klallam tribe rejoiced and a little book of poems was gathered. One year I walked, alone, the full length of that stream.

Elwha, from its source.
Threadwhite falls
out of snow-tunnel mouths with
cold mist-breath
saddles of deep snow on ridges —

o milky confluence, bank cutter
alder toppler
make meander,
swampy acres     elk-churned mud —

The big Doug fir in this valley,
deep grooved bark, it adapts, where
Sitka spruce often can't.
Three days on trail,

*— Trail crew foreman says they finally got wise*
*to making trails low on the outside, so water*
*can run off good — before they were worried because*
*pack stock always walks the outside of the trail*
*because they don't want to bump their loads on rocks*
*or trees.         "Punchin out all the way from N Fork*
*over Low Divide & clear back here, this punchin gets*
*mighty old"*

Puncheon slab saw-cut *wowed*

*"They got rip-cut chains now maybe different rakers
this here punchin gets old"*

About 12:30 come to Whiskey Bend.
That lowland smell —

### Charles Freer in a Sierra Snowstorm
### *(little did I know)*


Charles Freer made a fortune building railroad cars.
What he most loved in all the world was art.
He bought East Asian Art — China – Japan —
when things were cheap
and built a fine stone building for his works right on the Mall,
a lot's in storage, underground.

— After two seasons up on
Lookouts in the North Cascades,
a few years in Japan,
and many climbs on the snowpeaks of the west,
I found myself once in DC and asked to see
a sidewise handscroll mentioned in a book
"Rivers and Mountains Without End" or was it "Streams"?
kept at the Freer. I wanted to study
just how an artist might take on
the size of a range of mountains,
the landscape of the world.

They let me roll it out a meter at a time
and always kept an eye — allowed to write notes only with a pencil
— I think it was three hours.

Then slowly rolled the scroll back to the start.

## Why I Take Good Care of My Macintosh

Because it broods under its hood like a perched falcon,

Because it jumps like a skittish horse and sometimes throws me,

Because it is pokey when cold,

Because plastic is a sad strong material that is charming to rodents,

Because it is flighty,

Because my mind flies into it through my fingers,

Because it leaps forward and backward, is an endless sniffer and searcher,

Because its keys click like hail on a boulder,

And it winks when it goes out,

And puts word-heaps into hoards for me, dozens of pockets of gold under
    boulders

in streambeds, identical seedpods strong on a vine, or it stores bins of bolts;

And I lose them and find them again,

Because whole worlds of writing can be boldly laid out and then highlighted
    and vanish in a flash at "delete,"

so it teaches of impermanence and pain;

And because my computer and me are both brief in this world,

both foolish, and we have earthly fates,

Because I have let it move in with me right in the tent,

And it goes with me out every morning;

We fill up our baskets, get back home,

Feel rich, relax,

I throw it a scrap and it hums.

## Artemis and Pan

"The wildness of the savage is but a faint symbol of the awful ferity with which good men and lovers meet." — HD THOREAU

The "field" of the wild
            Ainu, *iworu,*

        feeling the field; outback the ears;
outside the eyes, faint whiff — loose knees

Two fluff gray-squirrel tails whip round an oak's
        gray bark
Wildly horny    ferociously aloof
        the ferity of lovers

Pan and Artemis
        bow-twang    or
        open-sight .270 barks a puff

bring down a deer
and skin it together
eat fresh liver
        cooked over embers


In the silvery light of the moon

## Anger, Cattle, and Achilles

Two of my best friends quit speaking
one said his wrath was like that of Achilles.
The three of us had traveled on the desert,
awakened to bird song and sunshine under ironwoods
       in a wadi south of the border.

They both were herders. One with cattle and poems,
the other with business and books.

One almost died in a car crash but slowly recovered
the other gave up all his friends,
       took refuge in a city
and studied the nuances of power.

One of them I haven't seen in years,
I met the other lately in the far back of a bar,
musicians playing near the window and he
sweetly told me "listen to that music.

The self we hold so dear will soon be gone."

## A Letter to M.A. Who Lives Far Away

Dear Melissa,
I do remember you
You had curly hair
And stood by the stair
Up there on Quadra Isle
With a shy smile
Say hello to your mother Jean
I don't remember your sister's name
And that's a shame
But I sort of remember her face
And natural grace
Not all poetry has to rhyme
But this time
I'm writing back, the way you did it
It's to your credit
You got me to write this form
Since real poetry is born
From a formless place
Which is our Original Face
Zen Buddhists say,
In play.
So if this helps you to be a writer
It will please your new friend
Gary Snyder.

24. XI. 1986

FIRST FLIGHT

## The Names of Actaeon's Hounds

Black-foot
Trail-follower
Voracious
Gazelle
Mountain-ranger
Fawn-killer
Hurricane
Hunter
Winged
Sylvan
Glen
Shepherd
Seizer
Catcher
Runner
Gnasher
Spot
Tigress
Might
White
Soot
Spartan
Whirlwind
Swift
Cyprian
Wolf
Grasper
Black
Shag
Fury
White-tooth
Barker
Black-hair
Beast-killer
Mountaineer

## Old New Mexican Genetics

Santa Fe, at the Palace of the Governors, this 18th century listing of official genetic possibilities:

*Español*. White. But maybe a Mestizo, or anyone who has enough money and the right style

*Indio*. A Native American person

*Mestizo*. One Spanish and one Indio parent

*Color Quebrado*. "Broken color" —a rare category of 3-way or more mix. White / African / Indio

*Mulato*. White/African ancestry

*Coyote*. Indio parent with Mestizo parent

*Lobo*. One Indio plus one African parent

*Genizaro* (Janissary). Plains Indian captives sold and used as slaves

## *Polyandry*

The following castes practice polyandry:

Nayars, Thandanes, and Thiyyas:

Kammalane such as goldsmiths,
Blacksmiths, carpenters, laterite cutters,
bell-metal smiths and braziers,

also the castes allied to those of Kolla-kurupe —

shampooers, masseurs, and leather shield-makers
bow-makers, leather workers,
astrologers, washermen and barbers,
exorcists and umbrella-makers,
herbalists and *nag*-worship songsters.

All follow patriliny but the Nayyars:
who are *marumakkathayam*, followers
of the mother-lineage,

from one end of Kerala to the other.

## Stages of the End of Night and Coming Day

Halving of the night
frogs croaking
cock crowing
morning and night together
crow cawing
bright horizon.
glimmer of day

colors of cattle can be seen.
sunrise
dew dries
cattle go out


— Antananarivo of Madagascar

# II. Locals

## Why California Will Never Be Like Tuscany

There must have been huge oaks and pines, cedars,
          maybe madrone,
in Tuscany and Umbria long ago.
A few centuries after wood was gone, they began to build with brick and stone.

Brick and stone farmhouses, solid, fireproof,
steel shutters and doors.

But farming changed.
60,000 vacant solid fireproof Italian farm houses
on the market in 1970,
scattered across the land.
Sixty thousand affluent foreigners,
to fix them,
learn to cook, and write a book.

But in California, houses all are wood —
roads pushed through, sewers dug, lines laid underground —
hundreds of thousands, made of strandboard, sheetrock, plaster —.

They won't be here 200 years from now — they'll burn or rot.

No handsome solid second homes for
Thousand-year later wealthy
Melanesian or Eskimo artists and writers here,

— oak and pine will soon return.

## Sunday

Well I know Sunday is Sabbath
but who ever does it?
Except Berry. Nice poems.
It just happens I'm free
the first time in weeks from
chores and promises,
cracked valves, late bills,
and I think I'll take time
to brush the dog. She likes that.
& oil dry hard leather for sheath for shears,
for the tape rule, hatchet —
read a recipe for an aubergine salad,
this isn't work —

Then go for a hike
toward the bobcat dens and gravels,
hope no wildfires start today
— I'll get there and back
and just for a second,
maybe play.

*Michael de Tombe*
*at the edge of the Canyon*
*the Killigrew Place*


The Michael Killigrew de Tombe place
on a fine ledge of land out over the steep south canyon
drops off to a far river roar through the brush
huge old oaks and once was a small worn house
where a logger and family with kids all lived and then left
A year-round spring on the slope up so high, welcome surprise —
Michael and Tove, Theo and Mike, Julie and Za
all made it work. With cows and chickens and gardens and ponds
and barn and studio, books and paintings,
all made again and again, and the grandfather's sword from Japan
the Emperor had given him!
Over the canyon, just down from Bald Mountain,
paintings of slopes and of clouds and the deep blue sky,
the echoing conch, the mantras, the smiles and the hikes.

Mad Michael a genius, a leader, a visionary English-Dutch-
Turtle Island Elder,
here in this room where he lay with his cancer,
his friends and his *mala*,
calming them, easing them, utterly sane

Utterly sane, and then slipped away.

## Chiura Obata's Moon

Walking along the noisy busy north Lake Tahoe shoreline highway 7 PM —
early October, late dusk, rickety houses, old motels
on the lakeshore side of the street a plastic
orange fencing keeps out
those who would try to get to the beach where they're building
some whole new set of structures for the tourists.
I'm at the Firelight Lodge, cramped for space and built around a pool
that's empty, the clerk a slender blonde with an accent,
Polish she says, but she's been here now for years
and plans to stay. She's pretty,
she knows the life of youth, in the water and snow world of Lake Tahoe.
Walking up on a sign says Sancho's Tacos, a tiny storefront in a house.
Off to the southwest planet Venus, really bright,
sky so clear and purple-violet tonight,
two pine trunks and that early crescent moon —
the silhouetted ponderosa pine mature and tall
I make my way into Sancho's — I hadn't planned to —
but it's got a menu more than tacos.
Three youthful outdoor-clad enthusiasts just back from
some ridgetop hike are laughing and drinking in the corner.
Sancho's an anglo! With a little beard and sardonic smile.
I decide to go for a dinner — a whole cooked tilapia,
never saw that on a Mexican menu before.
Shades of Jack and Nancy Todd. Some article 30 years ago
on the fresh water fish tilapia, cousin of minnows,
first from Africa, you could raise in your greenhouse in tubs —
the fish that might help all us back-to-the-landers
get virtuous protein, maybe feed the world as well.
Looking south toward the darkening lake and the murmur of
trail gossip just at my back, it's the right place to be —
The tilapia-rice-and-beans dinner comes hot and it's good.
Outside on the deck the moon and Venus have shifted:
I see Chiura Obata's woodblock of dusk at Yosemite,
dated 1930 — the soaring blue cliff, the pines, the new moon.

## How to Know Birds

The place you're in
The time of year

How they move and where in the meadows, brush, forest,
        rocks, reeds, are they hanging out
        alone or in a group or little groups?

Size, speed, sorts of flight

Quirks.  Tail flicks, wing-shakes, bobbing —
Can you see what they're eating?

Calls and songs?

Finally, if you get a chance, can you see their colors,
details of plumage — lines, dots, bars

That will tell you the details you need to come up with a name
but

You already know this bird.

*Starting the Spring Garden*
*and Thinking of Thomas Jefferson*


Turning this cloddish soil still damp and cold
with a heavy curved crofters spade

finally I've read the life of Thomas Jefferson
here we are about the same age
— eighty — except I'm living alone with my dog
and spading a tiny spring garden
and he had hundreds of workers
on the farm and fixing the house while he
mostly wrote letters and thinking — thinking
true democracy is to help everyone
do for themselves. Which means
we must think with the help of the whole
neighborhood, bullshit detectors in place but
cleanly and clearly forgiving
— to be free is to get past too much lonely stubborn
deluded private thirst for what?
for things? for some small perk?
So give and take. Where was Jefferson in this — I wonder —
whacking clods, tossing clumps of winter grass roots
                                        to the side
scooping out and heeling in some Asian aubergine
— the long thin kind you grill with grated ginger

Everyone free to decide to join in on the work
and the play
empowered to be free of "me"
in a world which both has and has not
hierarchy. But he had slaves
and never thought that through.

& Tom had friends like Madison and Adams
to honestly argue him down and explain
the cracks in his dream;

Now — out on the far west coast of the continent
this rough mountain pine tree land
two hundred years later,
putting another turn on
whatever he thought we could do
Tom Jefferson:          never too late,
never be through,
you always can pick up a hoe —

let your people go —

## Log Truck on the 80

Heading west down the 80
last slope before the valley,
pass a loaded log truck
incense cedars with that stringy bark
Mind watching lanes ahead
roams back to the mountains.
On the left side across the river
 out toward Forest Hill,
or back toward Duncan Canyon,
or south to Sailor Meadow —
dark forests pass in mind.
See a shady canyon, tangled gully,
under old pine and fir and,
there: the fresh cut stumps of cedar.


                    Someone napping with his chainsaw
                    after lunch

## Stories in the Night

In Native California the winter was storytelling time


Yesterday I was working most of the day with a breakdown in the system.
Generator 1, Generator 2, old phased-out Generator 3,
the battery array, the big Trace inverter — solar panels —
they had all stopped — cold early morning in the dark —
back to the old days, kerosene lamp — candles — woodstoves always work —
the back up generator #3 Honda, cycles wrong? Tricking inverter relay that
starts the bulk charge?

Big Green Onan — fueled by propane — wouldn't start —
(one time turned out there was a clogged air cleaner; oil-drops blow back up
from deep inside.)

(I try to remember machinery can always be fixed — but be ready to give
up the plans that were made for the day — go back to the manual — call up
friends who know more — make some tea — relax with your tools and your
problems, start enjoying the day.)

First fifteen years we lived here, kerosene lamps. Heavy tile roof in the shade
of a huge pre-contact black oak;

Cheri, Siegfried's long-time woman friend and partner, is due at any time
with a 9-ton truck of ¾ inch crushed rock. Wet dirt every winter eats up
gravel, keeping a few hard roads for drenching winter rains and melting
snows takes planning.      You have to ditch them too.

In 1962 going all through Kyushu with Joanne, walked around Hiroshima.
Busy streets and coffee shops, green leafy trees and gardens, a lively place.
But at Mt. Aso, great caldera in the center of the island, crater 30 miles
across, saw sightseers from Nagasaki with the twisted shiny scarred burn-
faces of survivors from those days. And then read *Barefoot Gen*.

What got to me about the Bomb was *too much power*.
And then temptation there to be . . . the first.

The first to be "The Empeor of the World."
Yet to be done.  So  change our course around, or there we head.

I could never be a Muslim, a Christian, or a Jew because the Ten
Commandments fall short of moral rigor. The Bible's "Shalt not kill"
leaves out the other realms of life,

How could that be? What sort of world did they think this is?
With no account for all the wriggling feelers and the little fins, the spines,
the slimy necks — eyes shiny in the night — paw prints in the snow.

And that other thing, can't have  "no other god  before me" — like,
profound anxiety of power and jealousy and envy,
what sort of god is that?
worrying all the time?
Plenty of little gods are waiting to begin their practice and learn just who
they are.

In North India, Fourth Century AD, some Buddhist Tantrick Teacher Lady
said, "That God called Yahweh to the west, he's really something. But too
bad, he has this nutty thing that he's
Creator of the world."
A delusion that could really set you back.

But returning to energy. I'll fix the Onan, give up on # 3, it's too far gone
and next time get a backup with a cast iron block and water cooling
and a warranty good for centuries — put in a bunch more panels for the sun —

The old time people here in warm earth lodges thirty feet across
burned pitchy pinewood slivers for their candles,
snow after snow for all those centuries before —
lodgefire light and pitchy slivers burning —

don't need much light      for stories in the night.

*III..09*

## Morning Songs, Goose Lake

Orion, Pleiades, in the east, then
white glow on the hills,
try to count the stars inside the corral of Capella
they fade as light from the east comes on

wild goose-calls  wake us  awake

crows, robins, woodpeckers      truck-rumbles
we diurnal daylight eyebright beings

hear goose-calls  greet the star-fade
far-off cows begin the morning  Moo.

Travelling to the Malheur Lake Wildlife Preserve in the Oregon
High Desert, slept the first night at a little campground by Goose
Lake on the Oregon-California Line. With Carole, Mika, and Robin —
August 1990

# SECOND FLIGHT

## Fixing the System

Under the topless, bottomless,
    empty blue sky
hands and knees,
    looking down a little hole

leaky gate-valve    drip drip


Young surfers on the
    frothy shallow beach
    ecstatic dogs bite waves
log truck rumbles on the bridge.

    Big River, Mendocino


Watching a tiny bird flit down and
perch on a standpipe hose bib
dipping drinking drops of drip

every valve
leaks a little
there is no

stopping the flow.

*"Reinventing North America"*

Living on the western edge of Turtle Island
in Shasta Nation
Whose people are Native, Euro-, African, Asian, Mestizo,
Pacific and Nuevo Americano — Turtle Islanders —
Where the dominant language is still Mericano
In the Homo sapiens year 50,000.

## From the Sky

        The sandhill cranes are leaving
soundings from the sky
songbirds from Central America
begin to arrive.
Flitting through the bushes
        snowpatches on the ground
truck still in four-wheel drive.

## Here

In the dark
(The new moon long set)

A soft grumble in the breeze
Is the sound of a jet so high
It's already long gone by

Some planet
Rising From the east      shines
Through the trees

It's been years since I thought,

Why are we here?

*30. VIII. 09*

# III. Ancestors

## Eiffel Tundra

Graceful. Several million rivets, as it arcs up a lath-work of steel riveted webs. The first level ascended either by the stairway or a slightly inclined funicular lift that has an upper and lower section to carry passengers in. Up to the first level, which has a full-scale quality restaurant, as well as a sort of "bistro" and some exhibits on the construction of the tower. Then the next level up another few hundred feet is a somewhat smaller area with outlook platforms, some glassed-in and another not; and a stand-up coffee place. From there you get into the direct elevator to the *sommet*. It's a fast elevator considering how much it gains, and at the top there are two levels. The lower level is glassed-in; step up to the next level and you're out in the wind. Above that is another 100 feet or so with a control room connected to it. A high mast is studded with electronic equipment, repeaters, what-all. When they built the Eiffel Tower they had no idea of what use it would be to electronics in the future. Everyone's bundled up, the usual complement of a few East Asians, not crowded but — these are hardy people! And I take my time to gaze down from behind the protection of a glass enclosure, out of the wind, on each section of the city — half an hour of studying each block and section while referring back to the map. It's nowhere a kind of a grid town although there are repetitions of the radiating star road motif, particularly outward from the Arc de Triomphe. This entire tower is repainted they say every five years.

> chill wind, air gray and misty,
> looking down on tundra, frost-heave-shapes, polygons,
>
> faint aurochses and mammoths browsing in the fog.

*Kill*

The women share in the kill

The women are first at the kill

The women kill the kill

Three straight vertical lines     tattooed


On the shaved plucked mons.


*pass through            go  past*

life, past death.


*Kalahari Desert dream, Botswana 1994*

## Claws / Cause
### for Zenshin Whalen


"Graph" is graceful claw-curve,
        grammar a   weaving carving

paw track, lizard-slither, tumble of
a single boulder down. Glacier scrapes across the bedrock,
wave-lines on the beach.

Saying, "this was me"
scat sign of time and place

language is          shit, claw, or tongue

"tongue" with all its flickers
might be a word for

sex, and       fate.
A single kiss         a tiny cause [claws]

— such grand effects [text]


*2000*

*Hai-en Temple South Korea*
*Home of the Total Tripitaka*
*Set of Printing Blocks*


Four a.m. sandy courtyard, Orion rising

The great drum     booms
from the painted bell-tower
     And the bell then bongs

morning sutra chanting
in the Great Hall up another flight of stairs
     & one more terrace further up the slope,
     is the hall of all
     the birchwood blocks.
     that print the thousand-volume *Triple Basket*
     Eighty thousand carved blocks rank on rank.
     Cooled by grillwork open windows

—one block page says it,

     "*live* the wisdom     gone beyond:
     consciousness     is shapely,
     being,  empty     formal;
     form,     is freedom,

these fast deep bows


*South Korea X. '00*

## Young David in Florence, Before the Kill

Michelangelo's David's not a warrior,
not just a clever boy — he's a cool young man.
Weight on the right leg, eyes left
brow crinkled, calculating, estimating
                    the text says Goliath is already down.

Left arm to his left shoulder and the stone-pouch,
right hand down at his side,
holds the ends
            long leather sling straps — he has *not*
thrown it yet.  Stands still,  in a deep place
a hinge in time

modesty
and naked grace.


*Firenze 2004*

## Mu Ch'i's Persimmons

On a back wall down the hall

lit by a side glass door

is the scroll of Mu Ch'i's great
sumi painting, "persimmons"

The wind-weights hanging from the
axles hold it still.

The best in the world, I say,
of persimmons.

Perfect statement of emptiness
no other than form

the twig and the stalk still on,
the way they sell them in the
market even now.

The original's in Kyoto at a
lovely Rinzai temple where they
show it once a year

this one's a perfect copy from Benrido
I chose the mounting elements myself
with the advice of the mounter

I hang it every fall.

And now, to these over-ripe persimmons
from Mike and Barbara's orchard.
Napkin in hand,
I bend over the sink

suck the sweet orange goop
that's how I like it
gripping a little twig

those painted persimmons

sure cure hunger


*(Dôgen: ". . . there is no remedy for satisfying hunger*
*other than a painted rice-cake." November 1242.)*

## The Bend in the Vlatava

On a stone bridge in Praha
watching water swirl and splash below
scouring stone millrace

darkly frothy,
thinking soon I leave and go,
this place for birds, this town,

all its stairs and walkways,
drains and gates
leading water to the river

sweeping toward the Elbe,
Hamburg, North Sea,
curving little river

I have seen your water
everywhere I walk
— your big wide bend at the Hrad —

> *I will remember you Vlatava River*
> *as I streak on winged sandals*
> *west to the rivers of home.*

## The Shrine at Delphi

The shrine compound is located eight or ten miles inland and about 1500' above sea level. Above are rock steeps. The hills are rocky outcrops and a kind of chaparral. Neatly arranged and lavish, extensive, "European Cultural Center" we stay at. Delphi oracle power lasted about 2000 years, finally shut down by Theodosius in AD 385.

A stream comes down a ravine reaching back to Mt. Parnassus, waters the "Castalian Spring" of pilgrim-purification. In a rocky cleft, a chosen place, I leave an offering from Turtle Island: a large quartz crystal, a *panaka* feather, a black-bear claw, a Bodhi-tree bead; and native tobacco. And chant the *Daihishu*. That night we share poems.

> I'm in the Tourist Guest House
> Together with Greek poets, teachers, writers,
> at the ruins of the Shrine of Delphi
> on a rocky slope of chaparral
>
> and a lovely young poet reads aloud
> in Greek translation
> my poems for you,
> takes me first back to Kyoto,
>
> the room in the temple by the old plum tree
> where one night I dreamed of you
> forty years ago
>
> And eight years even further back,
> to an apple orchard,
> us making love in the shadow of leaves
> curled up together, happy, green

I knew even then
I'd never feel quite like that
with anyone,
ever again.

*5.XII.98*

## Wildfire News

For millions,

for hundreds of millions of years

there were fires. Fire after fire.

Fire raging forest or jungle,

giant lizards dashing away

big necks from the sea

looking out at the land in surprise —

fire after fire. Lightning strikes

by the thousands, just like today.

Volcanoes erupting, fire flowing over the land.

Huge Sequoia    two foot thick fireproof bark

fire pines, their cones love the heat,

how long to say,

that's how they covered the continents

ten lakhs of millennia or more.


I have to slow down my mind.

slow down my mind

Rome was built in a day.

## Otzi Crosses Over

I concluded that he was crossing the range to get to a settlement on the other side where his daughter lived. He had unfinished arrows in his quiver that he could finish over the winter, and he'd return to the south side of the range next spring.

Moretti and I had spent the day in Bolzano studying his tools, clothes, herbs, flints, everything about him — and then when we were up on the Dolomite ridge near Sella Pass I realized we were looking far at the range he had indeed walked over — and it all fell into place.

### On his Way

He walks steady up the slope — bedrock and plant clumps — wind in his ear, beard waving a bit in the breeze — low clouds from the west in puffs — passing over and through the high peak points; blue sky gaps seen — farther on a set of white and gray cloud puffs hides a ridge. View through a notch to farther blue cloud-shadow patches and sunshine — breeze softens — getting into snow now, sun behind clouds but still lots of light,

Sore knee, and painful shoulder — but — about to step out on the icefield, cross it and go down the other side, more snow and rock and alpine fir below. This moment sun and wind — my little knife, my fire-kit, my settled daughter, this lonely route.

*4000 years ago. 22 Sept 2004.*

THIRD FLIGHT

*Inupiaq values*

HUMOR

SHARING

HUMILITY

HARD WORK

SPIRITUALITY

COOPERATION

FAMILY ROLES

AVOID CONFLICT

HUNTER SUCCESS

DOMESTIC SKILLS

LOVE FOR CHILDREN

RESPECT FOR NATURE

RESPECT FOR OTHERS

RESPECT FOR ELDERS

RESPONSIBILITY FOR TRIBE

KNOWLEDGE OF LANGUAGE

KNOWLEDGE OF FAMILY TREE

On the walls of a classroom in a tiny school in Kobuk Alaska just a bit south of the tree-line.

## Seven Brief Poems from Italia

*Roma*

Built back, of old stones from old buildings,
old bricks and stones on even older stones
— always-changing languages
broken tumbled talus slopes again

*Victory Monument*

Piled onto Roman Forum ruins
— dust on dust of days

*Roma*

*Acquapendente Forest*

Cowbarn on the mountainside
wooden hay-fork museum
life-size plastic cows in the yard,
"Michelangelo's Cow Sculpture Piazza"

*Tuscany*

*The Maremma*

Mesa-cliff edges of the lands of the Maremma
white cows, white horses,
fluffy white slow-walking dogs

*Pitigliano*

*Commercial Poplar by the River Po*

> pulp-for-paper groves
> so cool, so woodsy!
> cut every twelve years

*Isola Boschina / Woodsy Isle*

> Dense deep woods
> Creeper vines everywhere,
> over the Po    herons, and
> small hawk   *geppio*
> large hawk              *poliana*

*Po Valley*

*Alongside the Road just Below Sella Pass*

> leaning back on a
>> bench look straight up
>> at the blue sky duomo

> all the church we'll ever need

*Alto Adige*

## Askesis, Praxis, Theôria of the Wild

The shining way of the wild

— its *theôria*

is,  that the world is unrelenting, brief, and often painful

and its *askesis*,

cold, hunger, stupid mistakes, bitterness, delusions, loneliness;

hard nights and days                    are unavoidable

to find the *praxis* is to

hang in, work it out, watch for the moment,

coiled and gazing,          the shining way of the wild

*from before, & 4. IX. 94*

# IV. Go Now

## Go Now

*You don't want to read this,*
*reader,*
*be warned, turn back*
*from the darkness,*
*go now.*

— about death and the
death of a lover — it's not some vague meditation
or a homily, not irony,
no god or enlightenment or
acceptance — or struggle — with the
end of our life,

it's about how the eyes
sink back and the teeth stand out
after a few warm days.
Her last
breath, and I still wasn't ready
for *that* breath, that last, to come
at last. After ten long years.
So thin that the joints showed through,
each sinew and knob
Shakyamuni coming down from the mountain
after all that fasting
looked plumper than her.
       "I met a walking
              skeleton, his name was Thomas Quinn" —
we sang
back then
she could barely walk, but she did.
I gave her the drugs every night and we always
kissed sweetly and fiercely after the push;
kissed hard, and our teeth clacked, her
lips dry, fierce, she was all
bones, breath and eyes.

We hadn't made love in eight years
she had holes that drained all the time
in her sides, new ones that came,
end game — and she talked when she could.

Daughters, mother, sister, cousins, friends
in and out of the room. Even the
hardened hospice nurse in tears.

"Goodnight sweetheart, well it's time to go."
our duet, cheek to cheek,
for that last six weeks

She watched the small nesting birds
in the tree just outside.
Then she died.
I sponged her and put on a blouse
with sleeves to cover gaunt elbows,
a long gauzy skirt
like Mumtaz Mahal —

I was alone. Then they came.
One daughter cried out
"She's a corpse!" and stood fixed
outside on the deck. It was warm.
The third day
the van from the funeral home came for her,
backing up close to the door,
I helped roll her into the sheets
slid on a gurney and wheeled to the car
and they drove up the rough gravel hill
our family group standing there silent
as I turned, held my breath,
closed my eyes to the sky.

Five days of heat and they called me,
just Kai and me, to come witness cremation.
It cost extra. Only the two of us

wanted to be there, to see.
We followed the limousine
through a concrete-yard with hoppers of gravel
through a gate beyond that
to an overgrown
sheet metal warehouse that once was a body-shop
to the furnace and chimney room,
it looked like a kiln for a potter,
there were cardboard coffins
stacked up    empty around.

The young man at a desk and a table
filling out papers, sweating, as we
set out the incense and bell, the candle,
and I went to the light cardboard coffin
and opened the lid. The smell hit like a blow.
I had thought that the funeral home
had some sort of cooling
like a walk-in
maybe they did. But it didn't much help.
Her gaunt face more sunken, dehydrated,
eyes still open but dull, teeth bigger, her body,
her body for sure, my sweet lady's body
down to essentials, and I placed two books on
her breast, books she had written,
to send on her way, looked again
            and again,
and closed it    and nodded.

He rolled it up close, slid the
box in the furnace, locked down the door,
like loading a torpedo
we burned incense and chanted the
texts for impermanence and all beings who have lived
or who ever will yet; things writ only in magic
and just for the dead — *not for you dear reader* —
watching the temperature gauge on the furnace,
firing with propane, go steadily up.

*So now we can go.*
Maybe I know where she's gone —

Kai and I one more time
take a deep breath
— this is the price of attachment —

"Worth it. Easily worth it —"

Still in love, being there,
seeing and smelling and feeling it,
thinking farewell,

worth even the smell.

This present moment
that lives on

to become

long ago

# Notes and Acknowledgments

PART I. OUTRIDERS

*Gnarly*
Versions 2002 to 2012, then revised and sent to Glenn Storhaug for a broadside in Sept of 2014. Still in the works, January 2015.

*The Earth's Wild Places*
This poem was lost for some years and then turned up again. I don't remember any publishing history for it other than as a fugitive broadside maybe in the seventies.

*Siberian Outpost*
This poem was composed in the far southern high Sierra. First published in *The American Scholar* along with several others. Siberian Outpost is a bleak post in the ground along the Pacific Crest Trail, not far from Siberian Pass. There are no Foxtail Pine in Siberia.

*Elwha River*
The major river coming right out of the Olympic Mountains of Washington State. The Elwha tribe had been working for the removal of dams from it for years. Finally in 2011 the river was opened and salmon instantly swam the long distance to the headwaters. A longer version of this poem is with my unpublished 1964 notes for "Mountains and Rivers Without End." This version is now published in *Where the Thunderbird Rests His Head and Waits for the Songs of Return*, Kate Reavey and Alice Derry, eds. Sequim, WA: Rhymestone Arts, 2011.

*Charles Freer in a Sierra Snowstorm*
Published in *Catamaran*.

*My Macintosh*
This poem too lived the life of a stray cat for several years and was rediscovered by somebody at the *NY Times*. Like Sappho's poems it had apparently been used to wrap fresh fish.

*Artemis and Pan*
First published in Ann Kjellborg's *Little Star*.

*Anger, Cattle, and Achilles*
It always surprises me how many people in the audience know the name "Briseis"— the young woman that Achilles loved so dearly. First published in *Little Star*.

*A Letter to M.A. Who Lives Far Away*
This young woman lived on one of the islands in the Straits of Georgia in British Columbia. Since she had written a letter about poetry to me all in rhyme I tried to reciprocate. She was about thirteen then. She now works as a "Clown Adventurer Busker" in Vancouver, BC. This also was first published in *The American Scholar*.

*First Flight (for "flight" think of a set of wine-tastings)*

*Actaeon's Hounds.* As translated from Ovid's Latin by Frank Justus Miller.

*Old New Mexican Genetics* from the Palace of the Governors. On display in the museum.

*Polyandry,* from a book on that topic based on the State of Kerala in SW India.

*Stages of the End of Night*, from Madagascar.

PART II. LOCALS

*Why California Will Never Be Like Tuscany*
Published first in *The American Scholar*.

*Sunday*
for Wendell Berry

*Stories in the Night*
First published in *The American Scholar*.

PART III. ANCESTORS

*Claws / Cause*
for Philip

*Mu Ch'i's Persimmons*
Published in *The New Yorker*.

*The Bend in the Vlatava*

*Wildfire News*
Published in *Tree Rings*.

## Thanks To

An incomplete list of the many people about the planet who have been challengers, teachers, and friends to my various works —

East Asia —
My thanks to Bei Dao; Yamazato Katsunori, Hara Shigeyoshi, Bruce Bailey, Oe Kenzaburo, and Tanikawa Shuntaro for insights and conversations; and the great South Korean poet Ko Un.

Eurasia —
A special thanks to Irina Dyatlovskaya for her help in understanding Russian and Buryat visions of recent decades; Czech thinker and writer Lubos Snizek; Italian bioregionalist editor, translator, and farmer Giuseppe Moretti; the selfless and dedicated translators Rita degli Esposti and Chiara D'Ottavi, also of Italy.

Africa —
Julia Martin

The Spanish and Catalonian translator and tireless human rights advocate Jose Luis Regojo of Barcelona; Ignacio Fernandez of Madrid; Estonian poet Jaan Kaplinski who I finally met in Tokyo.

Mid-Pacific —
Shawna Yang Ryan

Turtle Island —
John Schreiber of Vancouver Island and the Chilcotin country; Jan Zwicky and Robert Bringhurst, a formidable team based in the Straits of Georgia;

Puget Sounders Kate Reavey, Tim McNulty, and Red Pine;

Columbia River people Jarold Ramsey, Bill Baker, Richard Blickle, Rosemary Berleman , and Ursula Le Guin; Deschutes country forester Michael Keown; and north coastal California sages Jim Dodge, Freeman House, and Jerry Martien;

Montana poet Roger Dunsmore and songwriter Greg Keeler;

Rockies linguist-poet Andrew Schelling, southern Colorado Rockies tipi-maker and beadworker Nosaka Kazuko; Southwest Plateau ethnomusicologist wanderer Jack Loeffler; potter and river-runner Joe Bennion; J B Bryan the publisher; scholar and jaguar-conservationist Diana Hadley; the guardian of the Los Angeles River Lewis MacAdams; rancher-poet of the southern Sierra John Dofflemeyer; Eliot Weinberger.

Right in the middle of it all: Wendell Berry.

Northern California —
Multi-faceted poet/actor/priest Peter Coyote; Brenda Hillman; the Grand Acharya of Mt. Tamalpais Matthew Davis; inspiring collaborator-artist Tom Killion; razor-sharp Rebecca Solnit; poet and explorer Dale Pendell; Robert Hass; and Malcolm Margolin with his tireless vision; precise and often hilarious Joanne Kyger; scientist-shaman-rebel Kim Stanley Robinson.

And always, Jack Shoemaker.